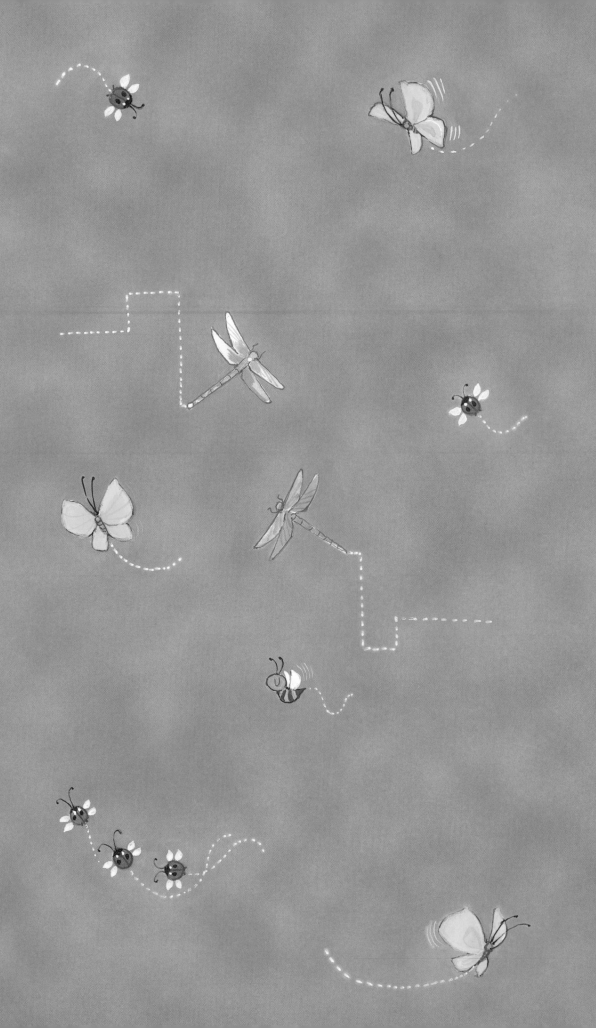

God created me!

_____

[NAME]

_____

[BIRTH DATE]

And this is my story. . . .

Children are a gift from the Lord.
PSALM 127:3

God Created
ME!

A memory book of baby's first year

Dandi Daley Mackall
Illustrated by Elena Kucharik

TYNDALE KiDS

Tyndale House Publishers, Inc. | Wheaton, Illinois

This book is dedicated to
the families God has chosen
to receive the blessing of children—
amazing gifts from God!

OTHER PRODUCTS IN THE LITTLE BLESSINGS LINE:

*Bible for Little Hearts, Prayers for Little Hearts, Promises for Little Hearts, Lullabies for Little Hearts (book, cassette, and CD),
What Is God Like?, Who Is Jesus?, What about Heaven?, Are Angels Real?, What Is Prayer?, Blessings Everywhere,
God Makes Nighttime Too, Rain or Shine, Birthday Blessings, God Loves You, Thank You, God!, Christmas Blessings,
ABC's of Blessings, Counting Blessings, Little Blessings New Testament and Psalms, Blessings Every Day*

Visit Tyndale's exciting Web site at www.tyndale.com

Edited by Karin Buursma and Betty Free
Designed by Catherine Bergstrom. Interior layout and typesetting by Kelly Bennema.

Scripture quotations are taken from the *Holy Bible*, New Living Translation, copyright © 1996.
Used by permission of Tyndale House Publishers, Inc., Wheaton, Illinois 60189. All rights reserved.

ISBN: 0-8423-3958-2

Printed in China

08   07   06   05   04   03
7   6   5   4   3   2

NOTE TO PARENTS

This book is designed to help you tell your child's unique story, in your child's own imagined words. By filling these pages, you will create a personal account of how God orchestrated people and events to bring about this birth, this life, this blessing.

As with most baby books, you'll be asked to fill in details for an accurate family record. But this story begins far in advance of the actual birth, building a sense of family history and heritage. Scripture verses throughout will help you and your child focus on God's love and personal involvement in your baby's life.

My prayer is that you will use this baby book to remember how faithful God continues to be to your family, and that one day your child will read and understand and praise God for that faithfulness.

Dandi Daley Mackall

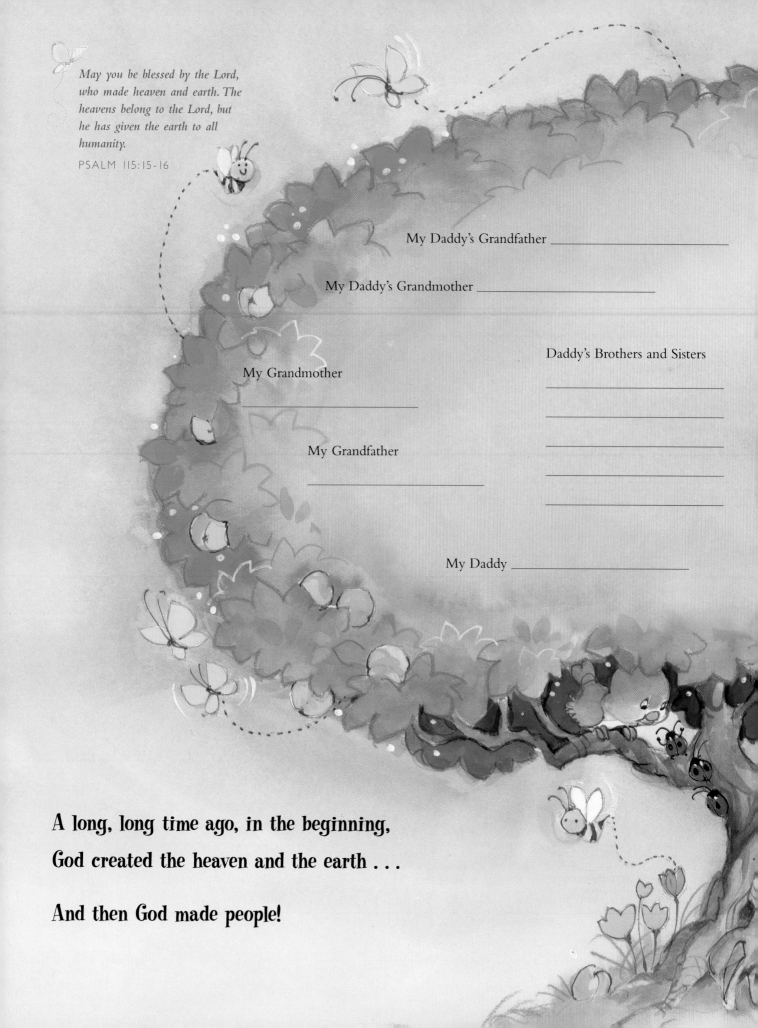

May you be blessed by the Lord, who made heaven and earth. The heavens belong to the Lord, but he has given the earth to all humanity.

PSALM 115:15-16

My Daddy's Grandfather _____

My Daddy's Grandmother _____

Daddy's Brothers and Sisters

_____

_____

_____

_____

_____

My Grandmother

_____

My Grandfather

_____

My Daddy _____

A long, long time ago, in the beginning,
God created the heaven and the earth . . .

And then God made people!

My Mommy's Grandfather _____

My Mommy's Grandmother _____

Mommy's Brothers and Sisters

_____

_____

_____

_____

_____

My Grandmother

_____

My Grandfather

_____

My Mommy _____

ME! _____

Your faithfulness extends to every generation, as enduring as the earth you created.

PSALM 119:90

Right from the very start, God had me in mind!

[PLACE PHOTO HERE]

[PLACE PHOTO HERE]

[PLACE PHOTO HERE]

You saw me before I was born.
Every day of my life was recorded in your book.
Every moment was laid out before a single day had passed.

How precious are your thoughts about me, O God!
They are innumerable!
I can't even count them; they outnumber the grains of sand!

PSALM 139:16-18

But before God could create me, God created my mom.

[PLACE PHOTO HERE]

MOM AT _____ YEARS OLD.

[PLACE PHOTO HERE]

And before God could create me, God created my dad.

DAD AT _____ YEARS OLD.

Honor your father and mother, as the Lord your God commanded you. Then you will live a long, full life in the land the Lord your God will give you.

DEUTERONOMY 5:16

When my mom was younger, people called her _____

Mom grew up in _____

and went to school in _____

Her parents' (my grandparents') names:

_____

Mom thought about being _____ when she grew up.

Her first job was _____

Mom's happiest childhood memory is _____

_____

_____

_____

When my dad was younger, people called him _____

Dad grew up in _____

and went to school in _____

His parents' (my grandparents') names:

_____

Dad thought about being _____ when he grew up.

His first job was _____

Dad's happiest childhood memory is _____

_____

_____

_____

When it was just the right time, God brought my mom and my dad together. They fell in love!

Love never gives up, never loses faith, is always hope-ful, and endures through every circumstance.

1 CORINTHIANS 13:7

Dad says this is how it happened: _____

_____

_____

_____

_____

But Mom says it happened like this: _____

_____

_____

_____

_____

[PLACE WEDDING INVITATION OR PHOTO HERE]

Then they got married.

When: _____

_____

Where: _____

_____

*This explains why a man
leaves his father and
mother and is joined to
his wife, and the two are
united into one.*

GENESIS 2:24

Mom and Dad lived
happily together.

They lived here: _____

_____

[PLACE PHOTO OF FIRST HOUSE/APARTMENT HERE]

How amazing are the deeds of the Lord! All who delight in him should ponder them.

PSALM 111:2

They kept busy doing lots of stuff, like: _____

_____

_____

_____

_____

_____

_____

_____

God filled their lives with blessings like family, church, home,

friendships, love . . . _____

_____

_____

_____

_____

_____

_____

But something was missing.

Someone was missing. . . .

[PLACE PHOTO OF MOM & DAD HERE]

I knew you before I formed you in your mother's womb.

JEREMIAH 1:5

So . . . GOD CREATED ME!

Mom found out I was inside her
and she was really going to have a baby!

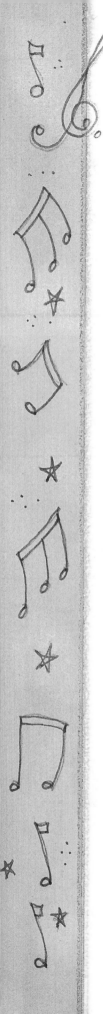

How Mom found out she was pregnant:

_____

_____

_____

_____

_____

_____

_____

_____

You made all the delicate,
inner parts of my body
and knit me together in
my mother's womb.

PSALM 139:13

Mom's reflections:_____

_____

_____

_____

_____

_____

_____

Mary quietly treasured these
things in her heart and
thought about them often.

LUKE 2:19

And Dad learned he was going to be my daddy!

How Dad found out: _____

_____

_____

_____

_____

_____

_____

_____

_____

As for me and my family,
we will serve the Lord.
JOSHUA 24:15

Dad's reflections: _____

_____

_____

_____

_____

_____

_____

_____

Pretty soon Mom and Dad told everyone in the family and many friends.

This is what they said: _____

_____

_____

_____

_____

_____

_____

_____

_____

[PLACE PHOTO OF FRIENDS OR FAMILY HERE]

God's ways are as hard to discern as the pathways of the wind, and as mysterious as a tiny baby being formed in a mother's womb.

ECCLESIASTES 11:5

[PLACE ULTRASOUND PICTURE HERE]

Everybody waited while I grew

and grew and grew inside Mommy.

Dr._____even took a picture of me!

The first time they heard my heartbeat was _____

The first time they felt me move in Mommy's tummy was so exciting!

_____

_____

Mommy and Daddy talked to me while I was growing inside Mommy.

They said stuff like_____

_____

_____

_____

You watched me as I was being formed in utter seclusion, as I was woven together in the dark of the womb.

PSALM 139:15

Mommy and Daddy waited and waited and waited.

Mommy tried to imagine what I'd be like

at 6 years old: _____

_____

at 16 years old: _____

_____

at 26 years old: _____

_____

Mommy wondered what I'd be when I grew up: _____

_____

She thought of lots of good advice she'd give me: _____

_____

_____

Mommy believed that the secret of happiness is _____

_____

_____

Mommy prayed for me a lot. These are some of the things she

said to God: _____

_____

_____

They thought about me, talked about me,
dreamed dreams for me . . . and prayed for me.

Daddy tried to imagine what I'd be like

at 6 years old: _____

_____

at 16 years old: _____

_____

at 26 years old: _____

_____

I know, Lord, that a person's life is not his own. No one is able to plan his own course.

JEREMIAH 10:23

"For I know the plans I have for you," says the Lord. "They are plans for good and not for disaster, to give you a future and a hope."

JEREMIAH 29:11

Daddy wondered what I'd be when I grew up: _____

_____

He thought of lots of good advice he'd give me: _____

_____

_____

Daddy believed that the secret of happiness is _____

_____

_____

Daddy prayed for me a lot. These are some of the things he said to God:

_____

_____

_____

_____

While Mommy and Daddy
waited for me to be born,
they got our home all ready.

[PLACE A PHOTO OF BABY'S ROOM HERE]

Here's my first address and phone number:

(Phone) _____

(Address) _____

_____

Unless the Lord builds
a house, the work of
the builders is useless.

PSALM 127:1

Even before I was born,

Mommy and Daddy knew they

wanted me to grow up with their values.

Here are some of the things they think are important in life:

_____

_____

_____

_____

_____

_____

_____

_____

_____

Dear friends, let us continue to love one another, for love comes from God. Anyone who loves is born of God and knows God.

I JOHN 4:7

And they kept waiting

and waiting and waiting. . . .

Some things were hard for Mommy to do while she was pregnant:

_____

_____

_____

_____

Sometimes Mommy wanted to eat strange foods, like

_____

_____

_____

_____

[ATTACH PHOTO OF MOM WITH BABY IN HER TUMMY!]

Everybody had ideas about what name to give me!

Names in the running: _____

_____

_____

_____

But Mommy and Daddy decided to name me

Full name: _____

because _____

_____

_____

_____

My name really means _____

_____

_____

The Lord called me before my birth; from within the womb he called me by name.

ISAIAH 49:1

Sooner or later, though, I'll probably end up

with these nicknames:

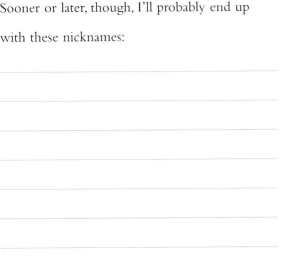

Other people were so thankful God was
sending me, they gave me presents!

[PLACE PHOTO OF SHOWER HERE]

[PLACE PHOTO OF SHOWER HERE]

*The Lord is my shepherd;
I have everything I need.*
PSALM 23:1

Baby Showers

GUESTS

GIFTS

GUESTS

GIFTS

[PLACE PHOTO HERE]

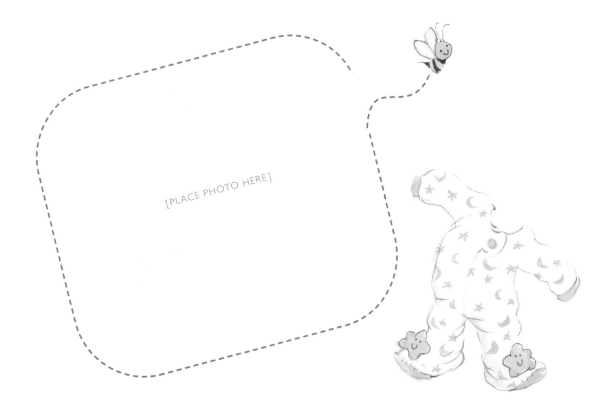

[PLACE PHOTO HERE]

GUESTS

GIFTS

Then God decided it was time!
My BIG DAY finally arrived!

Mom says it was quite a day!

On this day _____, I let her know

I was ready to come out! Mommy describes it like this:_____

_____

_____

_____

_____

_____

_____

_____

It will be like a woman experiencing the pains of labor. When her child is born, her anguish gives place to joy because she has brought a new person into the world.

JOHN 16:21

Daddy says it was quite a day, too! He describes it like this:_____

_____

_____

_____

_____

_____

_____

_____

You brought me safely from my mother's womb and led me to trust you when I was a nursing infant. I was thrust upon you at my birth. You have been my God from the moment I was born.

PSALM 22:9-10

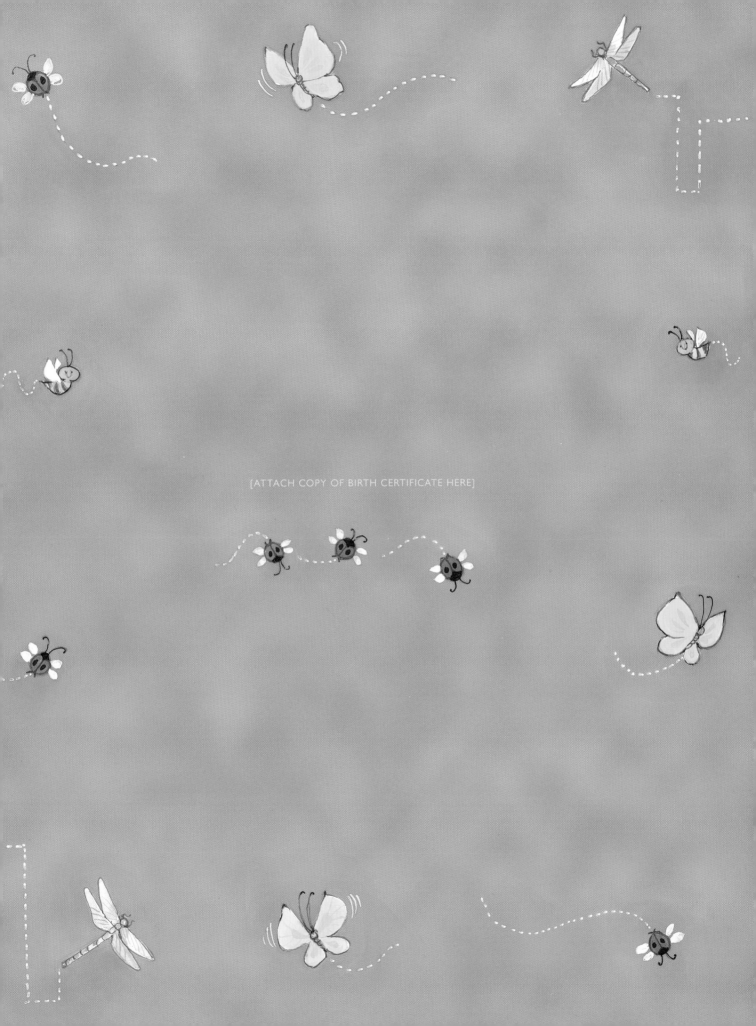

[ATTACH COPY OF BIRTH CERTIFICATE HERE]

Mommy and Daddy say there was never, ever a baby just like me!

Here's what I looked like:

*You made me;
you created me.*
PSALM 119:73

[PLACE BIRTH PICTURE HERE]

*We are God's masterpiece.
He has created us anew in
Christ Jesus, so that we
can do the good things he
planned for us long ago.*
EPHESIANS 2:10

Daddy says the first time he held me,

_____

_____

_____

_____

_____

_____

_____

_____

Children born to a young man are like sharp arrows in a warrior's hands.

PSALM 127:4

[PLACE PHOTO HERE]

[PLACE PHOTO HERE]

Mommy says the first time she held me,

_____

_____

_____

_____

_____

_____

_____

How we thank God for you! Because of you we have great joy in the presence of God.

1 THESSALONIANS 3:9

Here's how we told

everybody what God had done:

[PLACE BIRTH ANNOUNCEMENT HERE]

[PLACE COPY OF NEWSPAPER ANNOUNCEMENT HERE]

You are our pride and joy.
I THESSALONIANS 2:20

MY FOOTPRINTS!

MY HANDPRINTS!

[ATTACH HOSPITAL NAME BRACELET HERE]

Lots of people wanted to meet me!

Some of my first visitors were:

[PLACE PHOTO HERE]

This is what they said about me:

[PLACE PHOTO HERE]

Some people sent notes and cards to welcome me.

[ATTACH NOTES AND CARDS HERE]

It took a few days for Mom and Dad
and me to get to know each other.

This is what our first few days at home were like:

I ate at all times of the day and night!

[PLACE PHOTO HERE]

No one has ever seen God.
But if we love each other,
God lives in us, and his
love has been brought to
full expresssion through us.

1 JOHN 4:12

[PLACE PHOTO HERE]

O Lord, you alone are my hope. I've trusted you, O Lord, from childhood.

PSALM 71:5

I had my first bath on _____

This is what I thought of it: _____

_____

_____

Even sleeping was an adventure. At first, I slept (where, when, how):

_____

_____

_____

_____

_____

_____

_____

_____

The year I was born, some pretty interesting things were going on in the world!

The President of the United States was _____

and the Vice President was _____

My parents voted for _____

Other famous people in the news were _____

_____

_____

The world events everybody was talking about were _____

_____

_____

My family cheered for these sports teams: _____

_____

_____

Some of the best songs playing on the radio were _____

_____

_____

Mom and Dad's favorite TV shows were _____

_____

_____

And some of the biggest movies were _____

_____

_____

A few of the best books were _____

_____

_____

Most people liked to wear _____

_____

Newspapers carried some
pretty interesting stories!

[ATTACH HEADLINES FROM THIS YEAR'S NEWSPAPERS HERE]

I am leaving you with a gift—
peace of mind and heart. And the
peace I give isn't like the peace
the world gives. So don't be
troubled or afraid.

JOHN 14:27

Mommy and Daddy took me to church for a special celebration, just like Mary and Joseph took Jesus to the temple when he was a baby.

Friends and family who came were _____

_____

_____

Here's a prayer that was said for me: _____

_____

_____

Here's a Bible verse that was read: _____

_____

_____

Some things Mom and Dad will always remember about that day are

_____

_____

_____

_____

_____

_____

I asked the Lord to give me this child, and he has given me my request. Now I am giving him to the Lord, and he will belong to the Lord his whole life.

I SAMUEL 1:27-28

[ATTACH PORTION OF PROGRAM
THAT MENTIONS BABY'S NAME]

My church is called _____

and it's at _____

Our pastor's name is _____

Other people I look forward to seeing at church are _____

_____

_____

_____

The first time Mommy and Daddy took me to church, I _____

_____

_____

_____

_____

_____

_____

_____

God was so nice to us and sent his only child to us so we could become part of his heavenly family. So my family here on earth likes spending time in God's house.

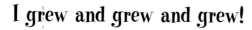

I grew and grew and grew!

GROWING-UP HEIGHT & WEIGHT CHART

Jesus grew both in height and in wisdom, and he was loved by God and by all who knew him.

LUKE 2:52

AGE	HEIGHT	WEIGHT
Birth		
1 month		
2 months		
3 months		
4 months		
5 months		
6 months		
7 months		
8 months		
9 months		
10 months		
11 months		
12 months		
18 months		
2 years		
3 years		

Health Record

VISITS TO THE DOCTOR

DATE	COMMENTS	IMMUNIZATIONS/TESTS

Allergies: _____

_____

Blood Type: _____

Special Notes: _____

_____

I trust in the Lord for protection.
PSALM 11:1

Whenever I got sick,
I got lots of care and loving!

GOD'S PROTECTIVE CARE

DATE	ILLNESS	COMMENTS

*Yes, you have been with me
from birth; from my mother's
womb you have cared for me.
No wonder I am always
praising you!*

PSALM 71:6

God looked out for me
no matter where we went!

ACCIDENTS AND NEAR-ACCIDENTS

DATE	INCIDENT	COMMENTS

He orders his angels to protect you wherever you go. They will hold you with their hands to keep you from striking your foot on a stone.

PSALM 91:11-12

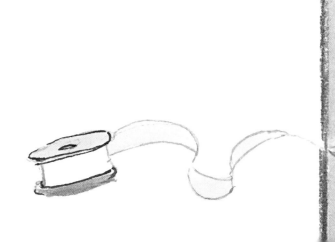

God surrounded me with VIPs (Very Important People)
who loved to hold me and play with me.

I loved it when my grandparents came to play.

We did things like: _____

_____

_____

_____

May you live to enjoy your grandchildren.

PSALM 128:6

[PLACE PHOTO HERE]

Here are other things I did with family and friends: _____

_____

_____

_____

[PLACE PHOTO HERE]

Make me truly happy by agreeing wholeheartedly with each other, loving one another, and working together with one heart and purpose.

PHILIPPIANS 2:2

God gave our family lots of friends!

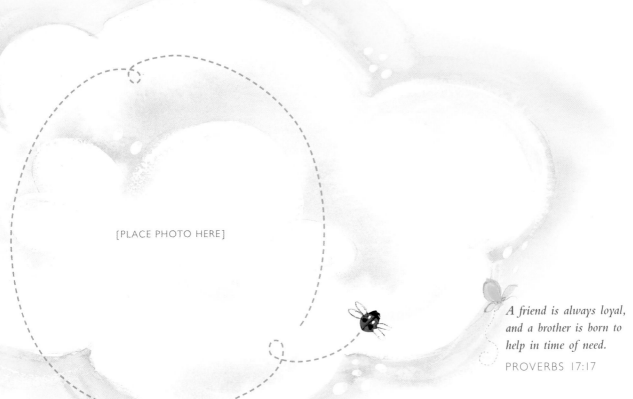

[PLACE PHOTO HERE]

A friend is always loyal, and a brother is born to help in time of need.

PROVERBS 17:17

Since I was a baby, just about everything I did was celebrated as a "first."

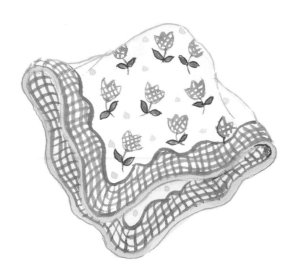

First smiled _____

First laughed _____

First grasped object _____

First slept through the night! _____

First held up head _____

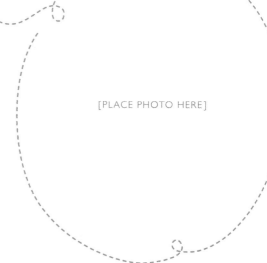

First rolled over _____

First sat up alone _____

First tooth came in _____

First ate solid food _____

First crawled _____

First stood up alone _____

First walked with help _____

First walked alone _____

First waved _____

First words _____

[PLACE PHOTO HERE]

First said *Mama* _____

First said *Dada* _____

First drank from cup _____

First ate with spoon _____

First phrase _____

First haircut _____

First plane ride _____

First boat ride _____

First train ride _____

First vacation _____

*Let your roots grow down into
[Christ] and draw up nourish-
ment from him, so you will grow
in faith, strong and vigorous in
the truth you were taught. Let
your lives overflow with thanksgiving for all he has done.*

COLOSSIANS 2:7

Pretty soon I had a bunch of "favorites"—things I really liked.

My favorite food was _____

_____

_____

_____

Every one of these depends on you to give them their food as they need it.

PSALM 104:27

My favorite pet was _____

_____

_____

_____

[PLACE PHOTO HERE]

You care for people and animals alike, O Lord.

PSALM 36:6

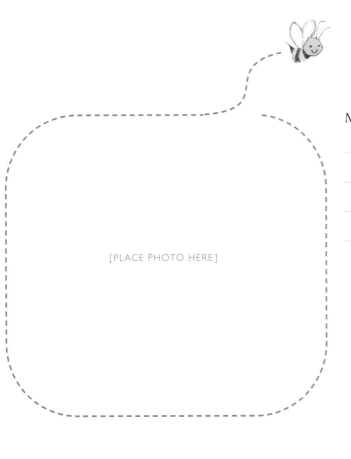

[PLACE PHOTO HERE]

My favorite toys and stuff were _____

_____

_____

_____

_____

Their trust should be in the living God, who richly gives us all we need for our enjoyment.

I TIMOTHY 6:17

Most of the time I liked to wear _____

_____

_____

_____

Guard me as the apple of your eye. Hide me in the shadow of your wings.

PSALM 17:8

My favorite spots around our house were _____

_____

_____

_____

My days were busy!

[PLACE PHOTO HERE]

I loved to do these activities and games: _____

_____

_____

_____

_____

On family car rides, I usually _____

_____

_____

_____

Praise the Lord; praise God our savior! For each day he carries us in his arms.

PSALM 68:19

I loved to have grown-ups read to me from my

favorite books: _____

_____

I have to admit, there were some things I just

did not like! _____

_____

_____

_____

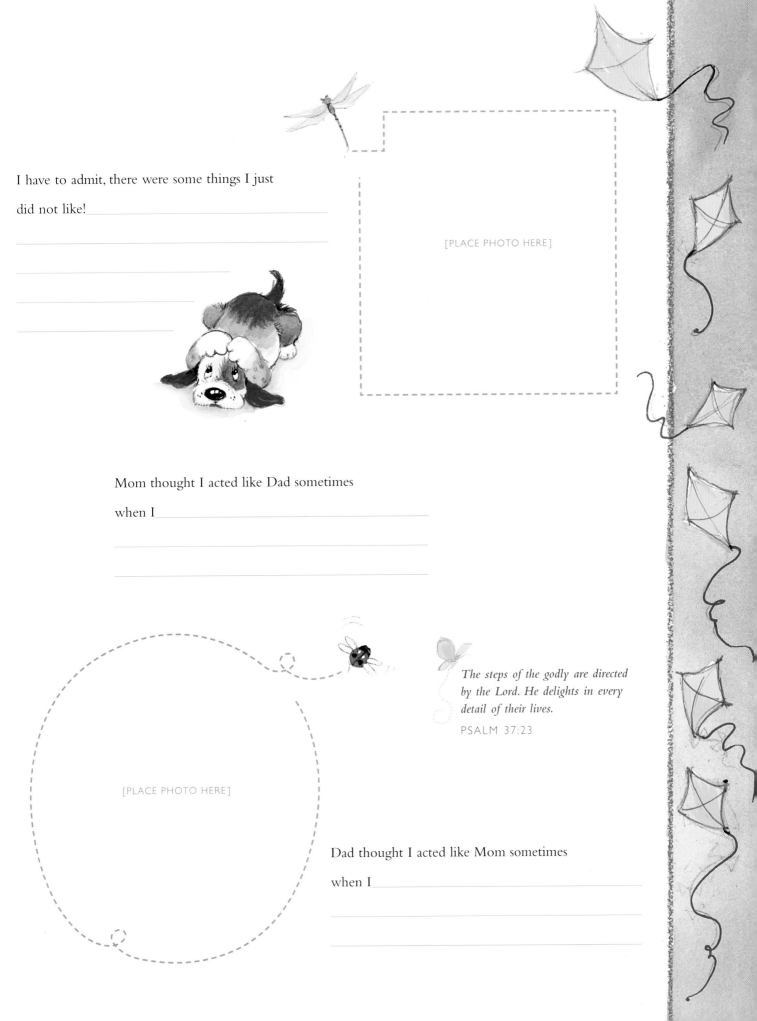

[PLACE PHOTO HERE]

Mom thought I acted like Dad sometimes

when I _____

_____

_____

[PLACE PHOTO HERE]

*The steps of the godly are directed
by the Lord. He delights in every
detail of their lives.*

PSALM 37:23

Dad thought I acted like Mom sometimes

when I _____

_____

_____

My very first Christmas was amazing!

We carried on traditions from both sides of my
family . . . and started some of our own. _____

_____

_____

_____

_____

_____

*God so loved the world that he gave
his only Son, so that everyone who
believes in him will not perish but
have eternal life.*

JOHN 3:16

[PLACE PHOTO HERE]

People gave me presents!

These were my favorites: _____

_____

_____

_____

_____

_____

*The free gift of God is
eternal life through Christ
Jesus our Lord.*

ROMANS 6:23

We celebrated the beginning of a brand-new year!

On my first New Year's Eve and New Year's Day, we

_____

_____

_____

_____

_____

_____

_____

[PLACE PHOTO HERE]

[PLACE PHOTO HERE]

Give thanks to the Lord, for he is good! His faithful love endures forever. Who can list the glorious miracles of the Lord? Who can ever praise him half enough?

PSALM 106:1-2

One of Mommy's New Year's resolutions was _____

_____

_____

One of Daddy's New Year's resolutions was _____

_____

_____

They even made a New Year's resolution for me!

_____

_____

We celebrated other holidays, too.

On my first Easter, _____

_____

_____

On my first Valentine's Day, if I could have given

valentines, I would have given them to _____

_____

_____

Love is patient and kind. Love is not jealous or boastful or proud or rude.

1 CORINTHIANS 13:4-5

[PLACE PHOTO HERE]

The first time I celebrated my country's birthday,

_____

_____

On my first Thanksgiving, we thanked God for

blessings like these: _____

_____

Then I will praise God's name with singing, and I will honor him with thanksgiving.

PSALM 69:30

Dad and I did some special things to say thanks

to Mom on Mother's Day: _____

_____

_____

Mom and I did some special things to say thanks to

Dad on Father's Day: _____

_____

_____

After a whole year, another big day arrived:
MY FIRST BIRTHDAY!

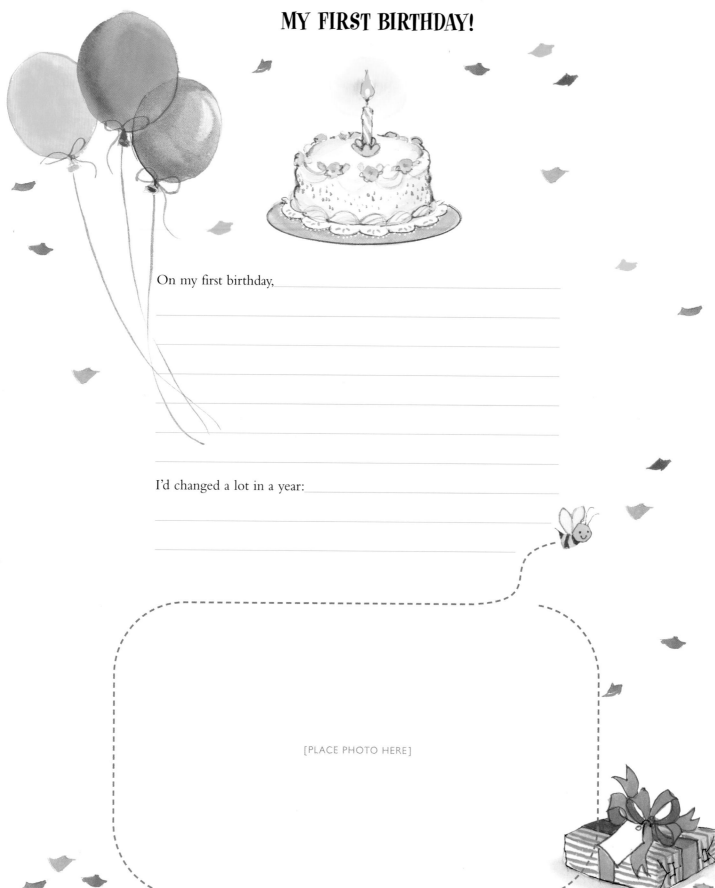

On my first birthday,_____

_____

_____

_____

_____

_____

I'd changed a lot in a year:_____

_____

_____

[PLACE PHOTO HERE]

[PLACE PHOTO HERE]

If you sinful people know how to give good gifts to your children, how much more will your heavenly Father give good gifts to those who ask him.

MATTHEW 7:11

My favorite birthday gifts were _____

_____

_____

_____

_____

_____

_____

_____

As Mom and Dad raise me,
God teaches them lessons through me.

My parents are learning that they have to be responsible for things like

_____

_____

Plus, having me for their baby is helping them get really good at being

patient in these areas: _____

_____

_____

Anyone who becomes as humble as this little child is the greatest in the Kingdom of Heaven. And anyone who welcomes a little child like this on my behalf is welcoming me.

MATTHEW 18:4-5

Mommy and Daddy are learning how to love me even when _____

_____

_____

God is teaching them all about forgiveness: _____

_____

_____

Mom and Dad are learning how important it is to talk to God every

day. Here's what Mom says to God about me: _____

_____

_____

Here's what Dad says to God about me: _____

_____

_____

I learn about God at home, too.

Mommy and Daddy want me to know God and his Son, Jesus, so we

_____

_____

And you must commit yourselves wholeheartedly to these commands I am giving you today. Repeat them again and again to your children. Talk about them when you are at home and when you are away on a journey, when you are lying down and when you are getting up again.

DEUTERONOMY 6:6-7

Mommy's favorite Bible verse is _____

_____

_____

Daddy's favorite Bible verse is _____

_____

_____

These are my favorite Bible stories and prayers Mommy and Daddy are

teaching me: _____

_____

_____

_____

_____

You have taught children and nursing infants to give you praise.

PSALM 8:2

[Jesus said,] "Let the children come to me. Don't stop them!

For the Kingdom of God belongs to such as these.

I assure you, anyone who doesn't have their kind of faith

will never get into the Kingdom of God."

Then he took the children into his arms and placed his hands

on their heads and blessed them.

MARK 10:14-16

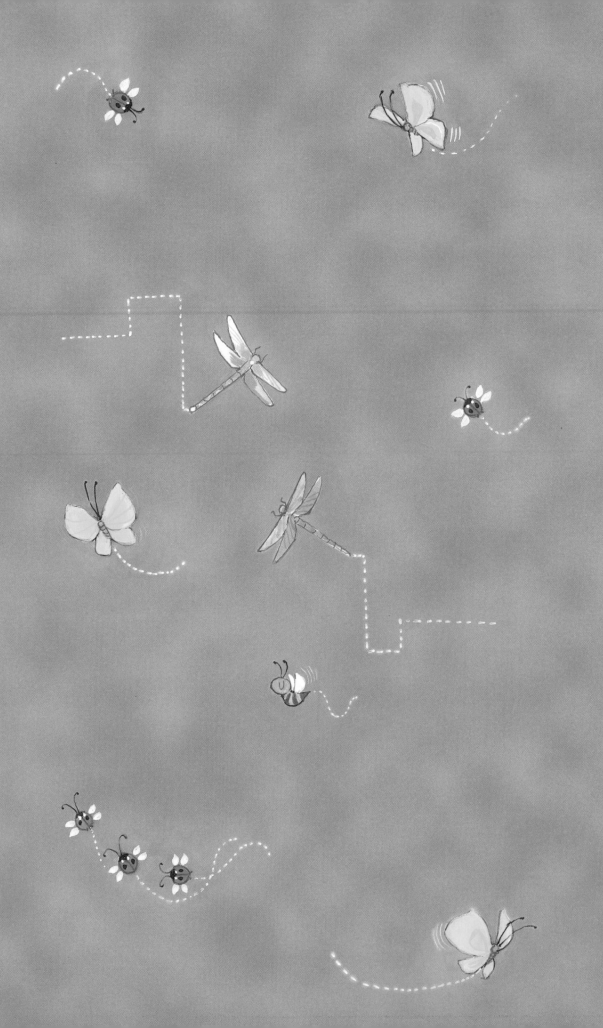